TARGET
Comprehension

4

www.pegasusforkids.com

© **B. Jain Publishers (P) Ltd.** All rights reserved. No part of this book may be reproduced, stored in a retrieval system or transmitted, in any form or by any means, mechanical, photocopying, recording or otherwise, without any prior written permission of the publisher.

Published by Kuldeep Jain for B. Jain Publishers (P) Ltd., D-157, Sector 63, Noida - 201307, U.P.
Registered office: 1921/10, Chuna Mandi, Paharganj, New Delhi-110055

Printed in India

Objectives of Comprehension

It is a fact that when students attempt a comprehension exercise, they are seldom aware of the purpose of the whole exercise. Many a time, even the guardians and teachers are not clear about the purpose. Of course, we are all well informed about the common purposes like comprehension teaches students to maintain their concentration level and to use strategies to enhance understanding of the reading material. Given below are some of the common objectives of comprehension:

- *Getting to understand the main idea of the text*
- *Noting the correct sequence of the happenings*
- *Recognizing the key words*
- *Making reasonable and logical conclusion*
- *Recognizing the genre of the text*
- *Distinguishing fiction from non-fiction*
- *Distinguishing fantasy from realism*
- *Recognizing the theme, plot and characters of the given passage*

What is it to monitor one's own comprehension?

Children should be trained to monitor their own comprehension from a very early age. While attempting a passage, they should read it again and again till its meaning is clear to them. They should note down the text which is not clear to them and try out to understand its meaning. They should stop regularly while reading and make sure that they fully understand what they are reading. They should reread and think again and again. They should read to the end of the passage, think sincerely and see if they are still confused. If yes, they should again read the passage and keep on reading till there confusion is vanished. They should learn the strategy of decoding multi-syllabic words and be able to summarize a variety of texts.

The series **Target Comprehension** is an excellently planned and graded series which brings together a diverse range of passages for the children to read. All the reading material that occurs in this series is judged on the basis of theme, language and the overall readability of the passages. The activities are graded and fit in justly with the passages.

Contents

1. Little Snow Girl 6
2. The Princess Mouse 13
3. The Story of Fidgety Philip 22
4. Tornadoes 28
5. The Tale of Two Brothers 33
6. Flying Fish 41
7. The Rabbit's Judgement 45
8. Christopher Columbus 53
9. A Rain Song 59
10. As Food Needs Salt 64
11. Gems and Minerals 71
12. The Magic Brocade 76
13. Telephone 83
14. The Boy and the Dragon 88
15. King Frost 95
16. The Tongue-cut Sparrow 101
17. Venice 107
18. Grand Canyon 111

Fun to Know

A warming up discussion
- Have you ever gone camping?
- Imagine you got separated from your team. What will you do to get their attention?

Little Snow Girl

Once upon a time there was an old man and his wife who had no children. One day, they went outside and watched other people's children making a snowman and throwing snowballs at one another. The old man picked up a snowball and said to his wife, 'If only we had a little daughter as white and chubby as this snowball!'

The old woman looked at the snowball, shook her head and said, 'Well, we haven't any child!' But the old man took the snowball into the cottage, put it in a pot, covered it with a piece of cloth and placed it on the windowsill. When the sun rose, it warmed the pot and the snow inside began to melt. Suddenly the old couple heard a lisping sound coming from the pot. They ran up to take a look, and there in the pot lay a little girl as white and chubby as a snowball.

'I am Little Snow Girl, rolled from the snow of spring, warmed and browned by the sun of spring,' said the little girl.

The man and his wife were extremely happy to hear this. They took her out of the pot and began nursing her.

So Little Snow Girl grew up in this household. She was a joy to the old couple. She was good and clever. Everything was going well for the old couple and their livestock. The cattle got through the winter safely and in spring they put the chickens back into the yard. But no sooner had they moved them from the house to the hen coop that trouble started. Late one evening, a fox came up to the old man's dog Zhuchka, pretending to be ill. The fox begged her whining, 'Dear Zhuchka of the white paws and silky tail, please let me go and warm myself in the hen coop!'

Zhuchka had been with the old man in the forest all day and she didn't know that the old woman had put the chickens back into the coop. So she took pity on the fox and let the fox inside the hen coop. No sooner was the fox inside the hen coop that it grabbed two chickens and dragged them off to the forest. Next morning, when the old man found out about the missing chickens, he punished Zhuchka and drove her out of the yard.

Poor Zhuchka left the old couple's house, whimpering. How sorry the old woman and Little Snow Girl felt for Zhuchka.

Soon, summer came and berries ripened. One day, Little Snow Girl's friends asked her to come for picking berries in the forest with them. The Snow Girl and her friends went to the forest.

In the forest, they reached a berry orchard. The girls were off picking berries in every direction within minutes. Soon, the Little Snow Girl was alone in the forest. She called out to her friends but no one replied. She started to cry. She tried to find the path home, but got even deeper into the forest. So she climbed upon a tree and shouted, 'Hello! Hello!' Soon, a Bear came crunching the dry branches and bending the bushes. 'What's the matter, my pretty one?' he asked.

'Hello! I'm Little Snow Girl. I came with my friends to collect berries but now they've left me all alone!' 'Come down,' said the Bear. 'I'll take you home.' 'No, Bear,' Little Snow Girl replied. 'I won't go with you. You'll eat me!' So the Bear went away.

No sooner had the Bear left that a Grey Wolf came to the Little Snow Girl and asked her why she was crying.

She told him how she had come here.

'Climb down,' said Wolf. 'I'll take you home!'

'No, Wolf, I won't go with you. You'll eat me,' said the Little Snow Girl. So the Wolf too went away.

Then, the Fox who had stolen the chickens came to lure the Little Snow Girl come down the tree but she refused to come down once again.

But the Fox did not give up. He began walking round the tree but the little girl would not go with the Fox.

'Wuff, wuff, wuff!' Suddenly, a dog barked in the forest. Little Snow Girl too heard the dog's barking. She was delighted to hear it.

'Hello, Zhuchka!' cried Little Snow Girl. 'It's me, Little Snow Girl, help me. The Bear, the Wolf and the Fox want me to come down from the tree to be eaten by them. I won't come down for them. But I'll go with you, Zhuchka!'

Hearing the Little Snow Girl's voice, Zhuchka soon reached her. Meanwhile, the Fox had run away hearing the dog's barking. Little Snow Girl then climbed down the tree. Zhuchka rushed up, licked her face all over and set off home with her.

As they passed, they saw the Bear hiding behind a tree-stump, the

Wolf skulking in a glade and the Fox lurking in the bushes. Seeing them, Zhuchka barked loudly, and they were so frightened that they dared not come close to the dog. In no time, Zhuchka and the Little Snow Girl reached home. The old couple wept for joy seeing their daughter and thanked Zhuchka for she had saved their precious Little Snow Girl. They gave her a nice saucer of milk and put her back in her old kennel to guard the house again. Everyone was happy once again.

 Let's remember the story

Answer the following questions.

1. How was the Little Snow Girl made?
2. Where did the Little Snow Girl go and why?

3. How did the Fox trick Zhuchka? What did he want?
4. What did the Bear and Wolf ask the Little Snow Girl to do?
5. Why did she refuse their help? Who helped her in the end?
6. What happened when Zhuchka bring back the Little Snow Girl?

Synonyms

Complete the following table by writing the synonyms of the given words.

Words	Synonyms
Promise	
Wrap	
Sick	
Afraid	
Warm	
Precious	

Practise writing sentences

Use the following words in your own sentences.

1. Chubby

....

....

2. Cottage

   ....
   ....

3. Pretty

   ....
   ....

4. Branch

   ....
   ....

5. Spring

   ....
   ....

6. Climb

   ....
   ....

Think and fill

Fill in the blanks using the correct articles, *a, an,* and *the*.

1. .... cat is sitting on .... sofa.

2. I had to wait for .... hour for Tim.

3. I need .... glass of juice.

4. My house is one with .... blue door.

5. She has .... apple and .... orange.

6. Mother took away .... box to let .... cat out.

Fun to Know

A warming up discussion
- Did anything strange or unexpected happen to you?
- What was it and how did you react to it?

The Princess Mouse

Once there was a farmer with two sons. One morning, he called them and said, 'Sons, you're old enough now to marry. But in our family, we have our own way to choose a bride.'

The younger son listened respectfully but the elder one said, 'You've told us, father, we must cut down a tree and see where it points out.'

'That's right,' said the farmer. 'Then walk that way till you find a sweetheart. That's how we've done it, and that's how we always will.'

Now, the elder son already knew who he wanted to marry. So he cut his tree in such a manner that it pointed to the farm where his sweetheart lived. When the younger son Mikko cut the tree, it pointed to the forest.

Soon, the two young men went their ways. Mikko walked into deep forest. There, he saw a cottage in the forest. But there was no one inside the cottage.

'All this way for nothing,' he said sadly.

'Maybe not!' came a tiny voice.

Mikko turned around and saw a tiny mouse on a table. Standing on its hind legs, it gazed at him with large, bright eyes.

'Did you say something?' he asked it.

Of course I did! Now, why don't you tell me your name and what you have come for?'

Mikko said politely. 'My name is Mikko, and I've come looking for a sweetheart.'

The mouse squealed in delight. 'Why, Mikko, I'll gladly be your sweetheart!'

'But you're only a mouse,' said Mikko.

'That may be true,' she said, 'but I can still love you faithfully.'

Mikko looked into those large, bright eyes and thought she really was quite nice for a mouse. So he said, 'All right, little mouse, you can be my sweetheart.'

Later, when Mikko and his brother returned home, they told their father about their sweethearts. Then, their father said, 'Tomorrow you'll ask them to weave you some cloth, then you'll bring it home to me.'

Next morning, Mikko went to the cottage, met the mouse and said, 'My father wants you to weave some cloth. But how can you do that? You're only a mouse!'

'Don't you worry Mikko. Why don't you rest while I work?' said the mouse.

'All right,' said Mikko, yawning and was soon fast asleep.

When the little mouse was sure that Mikko was asleep, she picked up a sleigh bell on a cord and rang it. At once, out of the many mouse holes all around the room poured out hundreds of mice. They all stood before the

table, gazing up at her.

'Hurry!' she said. 'Each of you, fetch a strand of the finest flax.'

Immediately, the mice rushed from the cottage and soon they returned in twos and threes, each with a strand of flax.

When enough flax was collected, they spun it into a yarn on the spinning wheel. Whirr...... Whirr....... Whirr......... Some mice worked the pedal, some fed the flax while others rode around with the wheel. Then they strung the yarn on the loom and wove it into cloth. Swish.......... Thunk..........Swish.......... Thunk..........Swish..........Thunk......... At last, the cloth was made, cut from the loom and tucked in a nutshell.

'Now, off with you!' said the little mouse, and they all scampered back to their mouse holes. Then she called, 'Mikko, wake up! And here is something for your father.'

Mikko sleepily took the nutshell. When he got home, his brother was proudly presenting the cloth from his sweetheart. Seeing it, the farmer said, 'Strong and fairly even. Good enough for simple folks like us. And where is yours, Mikko?'

Mikko handed him the nutshell. His brother laughed seeing it.

But as the farmer opened the nutshell, he pinched at something and started to pull it out. Out came linen, fine beyond belief. It kept coming too, yard after yard after yard.

Mikko's brother gasped with an open mouth and Mikko did too!

'There can be no better weaver than Mikko's sweetheart!' declared the farmer. 'Tomorrow you both will bring your sweethearts home for the wedding.'

Next day, when Mikko arrived at the cottage, the little mouse asked, 'Oh, Mikko, is this the day of our wedding?'

'It is, little mouse.' But he sounded very sad. 'But how can I bring home a mouse to marry? My brother, father, our friends and neighbours will think that I am a fool and laugh at me!'

'They might think so, indeed,' she said softly. 'But, Mikko, what do you think?'

'I think you're as sweet as any sweetheart could be. So let them laugh and think what they like. Today you'll be my bride,' said Mikko proudly.

'Oh, Mikko, you've made me the happiest mouse in the world!'

Then, to Mikko's astonishment, a little carriage made of nutshell raced into the room. It was pulled by four black rats. A mouse coachman sat in front, and a mouse footman sat behind. The little mouse hurried inside the carriage and the carriage took off. Mikko ran after it to catch it up.

At last they reached the spot for the wedding, on the bank of a lovely stream. The guests were enjoying themselves. But as Mikko came up, they all grew silent and stared at the little carriage.

Mikko's brother stood with his bride, gasping in disbelief. Mikko and the little mouse went up to him. But his brother with one quick kick sent the carriage, the rats and the mice, all into the stream. Before Mikko could do a thing, the current bore them away.

While Mikko was shocked seeing his sweetheart drowned, many guests gasped and pointed downstream. Mikko turned and to his amazement saw four black horses pulling a carriage out of the stream. A coachman sat in front and a footman behind, and inside was a soaked but lovely princess in a gown of pearly velvet. The carriage rode up along the bank and stopped right before Mikko.

The princess stood before Mikko and said, 'A witch had enchanted me and the spell could be broken only by one brother who wanted to marry me and another who wanted to kill me.'

Minutes later, a grand wedding took place with Mikko's bride the wonder of all though his brother's wife was also pretty. The next day, the princess brought Mikko back to her cottage—but it was a cottage no longer! It was a castle with hundreds of servants and there they lived happily.

 **Let's remember the story**

Answer the following questions.
1. In what manner was the bride chosen?
2. What did Mikko find in the forest? Who was there?
3. How did the mouse weave the cloth?
4. What did Mikko's father find inside the nutshell?
5. What happened when Mikko's brother kicked the carriage into the river?
6. Who was the little mouse? Why was she like that?

Practise writing sentences

Use the following words in your own sentences.

1. Farm

   ....

   ....

2. Forest

   ....

   ....

3. Cottage

   ....

   ....

4. Bright

   ....

   ....

5. Corner

   ....

   ....

6. Laugh

   ....

   ....

g) Circling the words

Read the passage given below carefully and put a circle around the describing words or adjectives.

The Arctic Region is one of the coldest regions in the world. Only a few animals like the Polar Bears can live there. The Polar Bears are the largest bears. They have thick, white fur which makes them difficult to be seen in their snowy surroundings. Interestingly, the Polar Bears' skin is black in colour.

They have two layers of fur on their bodies to survive the harsh winters and the icy cold winds. When there is sunshine, their skin absorbs the sunlight making the Polar Bears feel comfortable in the Arctic. They have small ears and tail and their big paws help them to have a good grip on the ice. Do you know that Polar Bears can swim for about 100 miles in the icy cold water at a time! Polar Bears can even swim under the ice to look for their prey. Seals are their favourite food.

Jumbled sentences

The words in the sentences given below are jumbled up. Read the words carefully in each sentence and then arrange them so as to make the correct sentences.

1. making/sandwiches/is/coffee/Mother/and.

   ....

   ....

2. Uncle/today/gone/fishing/has/Joe.

   ....

   ....

3. camp/his/brought/to/the/canoe/Fred.

   ....

   ....

4. dig/likes/to/baby/Earth/the/The.

   ....

   ....

5. up/flower/shot/a/bud/from/pot/The/small.

   ....

   ....

6. bird/Emily/the/to/the/songs/sat/of/listening.

   ....

   ....

Words and their meanings

Read the words given below. With the help of a dictionary find out their meanings and write in the table.

Words	Meanings
Mock	
Gaze	
Admit	
Sleigh	
Glum	
Astonish	

Fun to Know

3 A warming up discussion
- Have you ever been in trouble?
- What is the naughtiest thing that you have done?

The Story of Fidgety Philip

'Let me see if Philip can

Be a little gentleman;

Let me see if he is able

To sit still for once at table:'

Thus Papa bade Phil behave;

And Mamma looked very grave.

But fidgety Phil,

He won't sit still;

He wriggles,

And giggles,

And then, I declare,

Swings backwards and forwards,

And tilts up his chair,

Just like any rocking-horse-

'Philip! I am getting cross!'

See the naughty, restless child

Growing still more rude and wild,

Till his chair falls over quite.

Philip screams with all his might,

Catches at the cloth, but then

That makes matters worse again.

Down upon the ground they fall,

Glasses, plates, knives, forks, and all.

How Mamma did fret and frown,

When she saw them tumbling down!

(Heinrich Hoffman)

And Papa made such a face!
Philip is in sad disgrace.
Where is Philip, where is he?
Fairly covered up you see!
Cloth and all are lying on him;
He has pulled down all upon him.
What a terrible to-do!
Dishes, glasses, snapped in two!
Here a knife, and there a fork!
Philip, this is cruel work.
Table all so bare, and ah!
Poor Papa, and poor Mamma
Look quire cross, and wonder how
They shall have their dinner now.

 **Pick the correct answer**

Choose the correct answers from the multiple choices given.

1. What did Papa and Mamma tell Philip to do?
   a. To dance
   b. To behave
   c. To sit
   d. To eat

2. What was Philip doing?
   a. Rocking his chair

- b. Sleeping
- c. Eating
- d. Crying

3. What kind of a boy was Philip?
   - a. Brave
   - b. Naughty
   - c. Restless
   - d. Kind

4. Where were Mamma, Papa and Philip sitting?
   - a. At a restaurant
   - b. In the car
   - c. In the garden
   - d. At the dining table

Complete the sentences

Read the sentences given below and complete them with the help of the poem.

1. To sit still .... very grave.
2. Swings backwards .... horse-
3. Philip screams .... again.
4. Glasses, plates, knives .... tumbling down!

5. Cloths and all .... upon him.

6. Look quire .... now.

Prepositions

Fill in the blanks using the prepositions given below.

| over   at   in   by   on   across |

1. We will watch the movie.................. Sunday.

2. The bat comes out.................. night.

3. Grandmother will reach here.................. tomorrow.

4. The Leaning Tower of Pisa is.................. Italy.

5. There is a small bridge..................... the stream.

6. She swam..................... the river quickly.

Phrases, here we come!

Read the sentences below carefully. Some phrases which give you a sense of warning are part of the given sentences. Find them from the box and complete the sentences.

| let's not   be careful   what if   keep a look out |
| watch out   please make sure |

1. .... do anything that will get us into trouble.

2. Before leaving .... that you have the tickets.

3. Amy ....or you will cut your finger.

26

4. In the streets .... for the pick-pockets.

5. The guards .... for the robbers.

6. We must keep another pair of clothes .... we get delayed.

Let's hear your thoughts

What do you think happened in the poem above? Write your thoughts in the space provided below.

....

....

....

....

....

....

....

....

....

Fun to Know

A warming up discussion
- What is a storm?
- How can one remain safe in a storm?

Tornadoes

Wind can be a gentle breeze or a violent storm. As a storm it can uproot trees and electric polls. But do you know that wind can also move fast in a circular, rotating manner. This fast moving wind is very, very dangerous. This fast, rotating wind is called a tornado. You must have seen a tornado's picture in the newspaper or on television. But do you know how these violent, rotating storms are formed?

Tornadoes need a special kind of atmosphere to form. A tornado is a spinning column of air that is attached to both a storm cloud above and the ground below. Most tornadoes are formed from thunderstorms called super cells. They are formed when warm and moist air collides with dry and cold air. Low moisture conditions and strong winds are also some of the factors that contribute to the becoming of a tornado.

When these two air masses meet, they cause an unstable atmosphere. In an unstable atmosphere, the temperature decreases very fast as one goes up. As the warm air rises over the colder air, it causes an updraught. This updraught starts to spin if the winds are moving at different speeds and in different directions. The rotating updraught draws more warm air from the thundercloud, spinning faster. At the same time, the moisture in the air starts forming a funnel, which grows, moves down from the thundercloud and continues to increase till it touches the ground. This moving column or funnel of air is called a tornado.

Do you know that tornadoes are also called twisters? Tornadoes can attain speeds of up to 300 miles per hour. They are capable of causing large scale destruction. They can destroy large buildings, uproot trees and hurl vehicles hundreds of yards away. Each year about 1000 tornadoes descend to the ground. Only a few among them cause large scale destruction. The destruction caused by a tornado is a parameter to see how violent it was. In short the destruction done by a tornado is the means to know its strength on the Fujita Scale.

However, all tornadoes are not alike. Some look smoky white and some may have multiple vortices in them rotating around a common centre. Yet there are some that are invisible and their presence is made known only by the swirling dust on the ground. Do you know that tornadoes can also form on water and that they are called waterspouts? They are weak tornadoes but if they come on land they can cause great damage as they become tornadoes.

You would ask how long does a tornado lasts? Tornadoes can last from a few minutes to a few hours. No one knows what factors cause a tornado to disperse or dissolve. They just vanish into air after a while. You also might wonder where tornadoes are likely to form and when.

Tornadoes can happen at any time of the year and at any time of the day. They have appeared on almost all the continents but tornadoes are most likely to appear in the United States. In central US, an area called the Great Plains has the ideal conditions for the formation of tornadoes. More than 500 tornadoes appear in this area and thus it is also called the 'Tornado Alley'. Interestingly, tornadoes are most likely to occur between 3 p.m. and 9 p.m. These whirling, ferocious funnel can leave behind a path of destruction that can be one mile wide and 50 miles long!

People who live in tornado prone areas have underground cellars. They take shelter in these cellars when a tornado warning is given. After all it is not everyday that tornadoes take people to the wonderland land of oz!

Let's remember the story

Answer the following questions.

1. What are tornadoes?
2. Name a few factors that help in the formation of tornadoes.
3. How are tornadoes formed?
4. What destruction do tornadoes cause?
5. Why do we use Fujita Scale?
6. What is the 'Tornado Alley'?

 **Words and their meanings**

Read the words given below. With the help of a dictionary find out their meanings and write in the table.

Words	Meanings
Uproot	
Violent	
Collide	
Wonder	
Swirl	
Damage	

 **Antonyms**

Can you match the words and their antonyms given in the following table?

Words	Antonyms
Dangerous	Narrow
Increase	Small
Large	Appear
Destroy	Safe
Vanish	Build
Wide	Decrease

Word search puzzle

Find the given words in the grid given below.

tornado   super cell   funnel   twister   rotate   storm   cellar

S	C	E	P	R	F	U	R	U	L
T	E	N	T	O	R	N	A	D	O
W	L	L	W	T	S	A	U	F	E
I	L	E	I	A	U	F	A	R	L
S	A	N	S	T	O	R	M	A	U
T	R	N	S	E	S	T	S	L	C
E	S	U	P	E	R	C	E	L	L
R	O	F	S	O	R	T	R	C	H

Spin your own tornado!

Try this simple experiment in your classroom. With the help of your teacher, make your own tornado. All that you need for this experiment is two bottles, duct tape, water and some food colour if you like. Spin away!

Fun to Know

A warming up discussion
- Do you have a brother or sister?
- What is the best thing that you like about him or her?

The Tale of Two Brothers

'Stay away from those pots.' warned the elder brother. 'Don't touch them.'

'What are you talking about?' demanded the younger brother.

'Something about them bothers me. Why are they all upside down? I have the feeling that there is something magical about them,' explained the elder brother. 'We had better leave them alone.'

'Look, brother, we've been out hunting all morning and have not seen any game. Now finally we have come across these pots, and you say I shouldn't touch them. They might be magical. Well, I personally could use a little magical excitement in my day.'

The younger brother ran over to the row of pots. Slowly he turned the first one back up the right way and peered inside. There was nothing beneath the pot.

One by one, the younger brother turned all the pots. All were empty. Then, he turned the last one and let out a shout. Inside the pot, much to his surprise, was a little old woman.

She crawled out of the pot without saying a word to the little brother. Ignoring him completely, she looked at the elder brother. Pointing a wrinkled finger at him, she asked, 'Why are you standing there like someone who has seen a ghost? I'm just an old woman, and I cannot

possibly hurt you. Now, if you will just follow me, I'll show you something that is really worth getting your attention.'

But, the frightened brother wouldn't move from where he stood. She then turned to the younger brother and asked, 'Are you a coward as your brother or are you up for some adventure?'

The younger brother didn't need a second invitation. He followed the old woman who led him through thick bushes to a very large tree. 'Here's your adventure, boy. Take the axe and cut down this tree.'

To his great amazement, as soon as the first stroke of the axe hit the trunk, a strong bull stepped out of the tree. In fact, after each stroke of the axe, some kind of animal stepped out. When the tree was finally cut down, a large herd of bulls, cows, sheep, and goats surrounded the younger brother.

'These herds are for you,' said the old woman. 'Thank you for humouring me today. Now, take these herds home.'

Speechless for a while, the younger brother finally remembered his manners and thanked the old woman for her generous gift. He led the herds to where his elder brother was waiting for him. 'Just look at all the herds that old woman gave me!' exclaimed the younger brother. 'Now, don't you wish you had been brave enough to go with her?'

The younger brother explained what had happened in the bush as the two drove the animals towards home. It was a long way home. Soon, the brothers were tired and thirsty.

Then, as they neared a cliff, the elder brother cried, 'I hear water rustling!' He peered over the cliff's edge and cried joyfully, 'Water! Tie a rope around me and lower me down the side of the cliff. After I have had my fill, I'll do the same for you.' The younger brother agreed and did just that. Soon the elder brother came up, refreshed and satisfied.

Then, as the younger brother went down the cliff, he failed to notice an evil smile that had crossed his brother's face. The elder brother did lower him safely but he also flicked the end of the rope over the edge as well.

Greed had filled his heart seeing the herd. Then, he turned his back on his younger brother and started towards his home with the herds.

There was great excitement in the village as the brother entered with his herds. He told everyone how an old woman had given him the various animals. But his old mother asked, 'Where is your brother?'

'Hasn't he returned home?' lied the elder brother. 'He left in the early afternoon. He said he was tired and wanted to return home.

But the evening turned to night and then it was morning again without any sign of the younger brother. However, she did hear the singing of a honey-bird. 'This could be a good omen' she thought. 'If the village men follow this bird's song, it should lead them to the bees' nest for honey.'

Soon, several of the village men, including the father of the missing boy, set off to follow the honey-bird. Today, the honey-bird led them deep into the forest. After a long walk, the honey-bird started chirping loudly and flew around the men frantically.

'I think the bird is trying to tell us something' said an old hunter.

The little honey-bird led them to the cliff.

The father of the missing boy looked over the edge and the next instant cried, 'My son! The honey-bird has brought us to my son.'

In no time, the villagers made a thick rope of creepers and the youth was brought up. Then, he told the villagers how his brother had left him here.

'He shall be severely punished!' declared the old hunter. 'Greed would not be tolerated in our village.'

But before they reached the village, they learnt that the youth's elder brother had run away from the village. He somehow got to know that his younger brother was saved. As years passed, the younger brother, prospered and looked after his ageing parents. No news of the elder brother was ever heard.

Let's remember the story

Answer the following questions.

1. What did the two brothers find in the forest?
2. What came out of the last pot? What did it say to the elder brother?
3. What did the old woman ask the younger brother to do?
4. Why did the elder brother leave his younger brother behind?
5. What lie did the elder brother tell his parents?
6. How did the villagers find the younger brother? Who helped them?

Prefixes and suffixes

Given below are a few prefixes and suffixes along with a number of words. Use them together to make new words.

-ing	dis-	-tion	im-
build act	proper	possible	cry dictate
bark able	arm	age	fly cap
agree appear	ask	quest	pair

....

....

....

....

38

....

....

Dialogue writing

Mother: Are you going to play, Amy?

Amy: Yes, in a minute.

Mother: When will you come back?

Amy: Mother, I will come back before sunset.

Read the discussion given above. They are called dialogues. Can you write a small dialogue with your mother about going to the supermarket and a dialogue with your father about buying a new pair of shoes?

Practise writing sentences

Use the following words in your own sentences.

1. Surprise

   ....

   ....

2. Ghost

   ....

   ....

3. Adventure

   ....

   ....

4. Thirsty

   ....

   ....

5. Rope

   ....

   ....

6. Smile

   ....

   ....

Fun to Know

A warming up discussion
- How many kinds of fish do you know about?
- What is the most amazing thing that a fish can do?

Flying Fish

Have you ever heard of a fish that flies in the air? You would say that fish don't fly but swim. But the Flying Fish do fly or at least try to! Flying Fish are found in the warm oceans of the world. These small fishes have a shiny, streamlined and torpedo shaped body. The shape of these fish helps them gather enough speed to break through the water surface and become airborne.

These small fish have wing-like pectoral fins. These large wings help these fish to glide over the water surface for a long time. This ability to glide or fly also saves their lives. Flying Fish have lots of predators including tuna, swordfish and marlin among many others. Perhaps they have adapted themselves in this marvellous manner to escape from their predators. Interestingly, there are about 40 different species of Flying Fish!

The Flying Fish have large pectoral fins that resemble wings. Their tails are also unevenly forked and their lower lobe is longer than the upper lobe. Some species of these fish also have enlarged pelvic fins. These species of fish are called four Winged Flying Fish.

Their ability to glide over water is truly remarkable. In order to glide or fly over the water surface, the Flying Fish gradually reach great speeds. Do you know that these fish can attain a speed of 60 kilometres per hour! In order to attain great speed, the fish keeps its wings close to its body. Once they have attained the required speed, they need to break the surface of water. Then angling upwards, the Flying Fish breaks the water surface and at the same time begins to rapidly beat its forked tail which is still beneath the surface. It then also spreads its large pectoral fins to glide. And then, it breaks through the surface of water completely.

Amazingly, these fish can reach heights of up to four metres when they glide. Do you know that Flying Fish can fly for long distances, sometimes up to 400 metres! Once it nears the water surface again, it can flap its tail without completely returning to the water surface.

Flying Fish chiefly eats tiny organisms called planktons. Like other sea creatures, Flying Fish are also attracted to light. And so fishermen take advantage of this in order to capture them. Fishermen use canoes which are filled with some water. This water is not enough that the Flying Fish once caught can propel themselves out. A small light is also attached to the canoes, especially at night to attract the Flying Fish. Flying Fish are eaten with great delight in some countries though these fish are not endangered.

Sometimes sailors even find Flying Fish on the decks of their ships in the morning as they glide high in the ocean attracted by the lights of the ship. Do you know that some Flying Fish are also found in coral reefs!

So now you believe that fish can fly too!

Let's remember the story

Answer the following questions.

1. How do Flying Fish look like?
2. Do Flying Fish actually fly? Explain.
3. Name some predators of the Flying Fish.
4. How do these fish gain speed?
5. What are Flying Fish attracted to?
6. How do fishermen catch the Flying Fish?

Think and fill

Fill in the blanks using the correct articles, *a, an,* and *the*.

1. The dog is playing in .... park.
2. Bill got .... A in English.
3. Do you like to ride .... bus?
4. I live in .... United Kingdom.
5. I will like to eat .... pizza.
6. Karen ran after .... butterfly.

Complete the sentences

Fill in the sentences choosing the correct words.

| Light coral plankton glides forked predators |

1. The Flying Fish................. over the water.

2. It easily escapes from its............................

3. Flying Fish have a.................. tail.

4. It eats tiny organisms called..........................

5. It is attracted to......................

6. Flying Fish also live in........................ reefs.

Find friends

You are familiar with similar sounding words called rhyming words. Read the words in Column A aloud and write a similar sounding word in front of it in Column B.

Column A	Column B
Fly	
Swim	
Wing	
Fin	
Speed	
Delight	

Explore more!

Just like the Flying Fish, there is an insect called the Water Strider. It is interesting to know about it. With the help of your teacher find out why this insect is special.

Fun to Know

A warming up discussion
- Why should we help others?
- Did you help anyone? How?

The Rabbit's Judgement

Long, long ago, plants and animals could speak too. It was during this time that one day, a tiger was wandering in the forest in search of food. Suddenly, the ground under his feet gave way and before the tiger could understand what was happening, he had fallen into a deep pit. He tried over and over to get out but the walls were too steep for him to climb. Also, since he had not eaten anything for days, he was unable to jump high and come out of the pit. He called for help but none came.

Night passed. The next morning, again the tiger called for help until he was hoarse. Hungry and exhausted he slumped down on the ground, thinking that he was doomed to die in the pit. Suddenly, he heard footsteps near the pit.

'Help! Help!' cried the tiger desperately.

The next instant a man looked over the side of the pit and saw the tiger.

'Please! Please help me out of here!' pleaded the tiger. 'If you help me, I won't forget you as long as I live.'

The man felt sorry for the tiger but he said 'I would like to help you but, I'm sorry, the thought of what might happen once you are out makes me refuse. Please forgive me. I must be on my way.'

'No! No! Please don't think like that! Please help me!' cried the tiger. The man stopped hearing the tiger's cries. 'You don't have to worry! I promise! I won't hurt you! Please help me out! Please! I beg you! If you get me out. I'll be forever grateful to you! Please!'

'Wait a moment,' said the man filled with pity and began looking around. Near a tree he found a log. He dragged the log to the pit and then carefully placed one end of it in the pit. Then, he said, 'Here, climb up this log.'

Without any hesitation, the tiger climbed up the log and came face to face with the man. But no sooner had he been saved that he looked cunningly at the man and began circling him.

'Hey! Wait a minute! Didn't you promise not to hurt me? Is this your idea of gratefulness? Is this how you repay a kindness?' cried the troubled man.

'What do I care about a promise when I'm starving! I haven't eaten for days!' said the tiger as he came closer to the man.

'Wait! Wait!' cried the man. 'Let's ask that pine tree if it is right for you to eat me.'

'All right,' said the tiger. 'But after we ask, I'm going to eat you. I'm awfully hungry.'

Together, they went to the pine tree and explained the situation to the tree.

'What do men know about gratefulness?' said the pine tree after listening to them. 'Why your kind take our leaves and limbs to make fires to heat your homes and cook your food. They also cut us down to make timber and planks for your houses and furniture. Moreover, it was a man that dug that pit. Indeed! Don't give it another thought, Tiger. You just go ahead and satisfy your hunger!'

'Now what do you think of that?' asked the tiger, smacking his lips loudly.

Just at that moment, an ox came by. 'Wait! Wait!' cried the man seeing him. 'Let's ask that ox to judge?'

Again, they explained everything to the ox and asked his opinion on the matter.

'Well, as far as I'm concerned,' said the ox, turning to the tiger. 'You should eat him up! You see from the time we're born we oxen work diligently for men. We carry heavy loads on our backs and plow up the ground so they can grow food. But what do they do when we're old? They kill us and eat our flesh and use our hides to make all kinds of things. So don't be grateful to a man.'

'See! Everyone agrees. Now get ready to die,' said the tiger, crouching to pounce on the man. But suddenly a rabbit came hopping by.

'Please give me one last chance,' begged the man. 'Let's ask that rabbit to judge whether I should be eaten or not.'

So yet again the tiger and the man told the rabbit their story. The rabbit listened carefully. Then he said slowly, 'If I am to make a wise judgement we should return to that pit. So lead the way.'

So the tiger and the man led the rabbit to the pit.

'Well it certainly is deep,' said the rabbit as he looked down into the pit. 'Let's see, the tiger was down there and you were standing here like this?' he asked them. 'Well, get in the positions you were in at the time.'

Without wasting time, the tiger jumped down into the pit. At once, the rabbit took the log out of the pit. The man again peered over the edge of the pit.

'So that is how the two of you were. Now I can judge. The problem started when this man helped the tiger out of this pit,' said the rabbit. 'As I see it, there wouldn't have been any problem if the man had not shown kindness to the tiger. So I think that the man should continue his journey and the tiger should remain in the pit.' Saying so, the rabbit hopped away. The man too walked on while the tiger remained in the pit.

Let's remember the story

Answer the following questions.

1. Explain the phrase 'the ground beneath his feet gave way'.

2. What did the tiger promise the man?
3. In what manner did the man help the tiger get out of the pit?
4. Why did the pine tree think that the tiger should eat the man?
5. What did the ox say?
6. What must the tiger and the man do before the rabbit could give his judgement?

 **Pick the correct answer**

Choose the correct answers from the multiple choices given.

1. Where did the tiger fall?

    a. In a pit

    b. In a well

    c. In a tub

    d. In the river

2. Why did the man refuse to help the lion?

    a. He was afraid of the tiger

    b. He had dug the pit to catch the tiger

    c. He was angry with the tiger

    d. He knew that the tiger will eat him

3. The Pine Tree said that men were

    a. Unhappy

    b. Unconscious

c. Ungrateful

   d. Foolish

4. The rabbit played a trick to...

   a. Save the tiger

   b. Make himself look important

   c. Save the man

   d. To see the pit

Punctuation

Read the following sentences given below. Use the capital letters, commas, full stops and question marks in these sentences wherever required. Then write the sentences in the space provided.

1. where has mother gone

   ....

2. the child slipped fell and hurt himself

   ....

3. i had bread cheese and milk for breakfast

   ....

4. father has gone to paris

   ....

5. i study in st. vincent public school

   ....

6. i cannot swim but i can play tennis

   ....

7. madagascar is a country in Africa

   ....

8. the giraffe is the tallest animal in the world

   ....

💬 In your opinion!

In the story, the rabbit judged in favour of the man. Why do you think the rabbit acted in this manner? Write the reason for the rabbit's judgement in a few lines.

....

....

....

....

....

....

....

....

Practise writing sentences

Use the following words in your own sentences.

1. Deep

   ....

2. Steep

   ....

3. Refuse

   ....

4. Afraid

   ....

5. Smack

   ....

6. Edge

   ....

Fun to Know

A warming up discussion
- What do you dream about?
- Does your dream have something to do with what you want to do?

Christopher Columbus

How far have you travelled? Have you ever wanted to go around the world and meet new people and explore new lands? Christopher Columbus certainly wanted to explore the world since he was a child. He did fulfil his dream when he grew up.

Columbus was born in 1451 in Genoa in Italy. Genoa was a busy port in Italy. Little is known about his childhood and education but we do know that his father was a wool merchant and a weaver. His father knew that they could get rich by trade. It was with the same ambition, to get rich that Columbus grew up along with his brother Bartholomew. The times that he lived in were exciting as new ideas and discoveries were being made in Europe. As a result new lands were being explored and maps of the world were again and again been made. Adventurers were travelling around the world to places that were unknown before.

When Columbus grew up, he went to Lisbon in Portugal to work as a trader. It was in Lisbon that Columbus learnt to make maps and how to navigate a ship. As he learnt, he got to know that China, India and the East Indies were prosperous. He also learnt that people were trying to find a less dangerous and a shorter sea route to the East to trade with Asia, where the riches were. He and his brother thus decided to travel to China, India and the East Indies to become rich. But he had no finance for the journey.

But before, he arranged for the finance to support his journey, he studied the world maps present at that time. According to the maps, the world oceans were not as big as they seemed. Also, Columbus concluded that it was a shorter way to reach Asia if he sailed towards the West to reach Asia. So now that he had decided his route he decided to settle his finances.

But it was no easy task for Columbus to arrange the finances. He travelled across Europe meeting rich people for seven years but they thought his journey to be foolish. At last King Ferdinand and Queen Isabella of Spain agreed to give him finances. Columbus was delighted. He promised that they would soon have more lands to rule and more gold and riches with them.

Columbus set sail on 3 August 1492. He had three ships with him: the Niña, the Pinta and the Santa Maria. These ships were wooden, with sails and about 90 sailors worked on those ships. Food for the voyage was kept in the ship's hold. The men took salted fish in barrels, cheese, wine, water and chickens.

Columbus used a compass to help him navigate. He used a traverse board to mark the direction they wanted to sail in.

Columbus had thought that the voyage to Asia through the Atlantic Ocean would take only a few days. But in no time, the days turned into weeks and yet there was no land in sight. Columbus was troubled because the sailors, who were scared and angry, had threatened him to return if they saw no land in the next two days. Then, on the second night, a sailor on the Pinta saw land. 'Land!' he shouted. On 12 October 1492, Columbus and his sailors went on the island. Columbus called the island San Salvador. It was in the Bahamas.

He went on to sail to Cuba and Hispaniola. There he met the natives who lived there and realised that he had fulfilled his dream. But how mistaken was he for he had not discovered Asia but North America. But no one could tell him that.

Besides, before returning to Spain, Columbus claimed the islands of the natives for Spain!

Only two ships managed to return to Spain as Santa Maria was wrecked. Columbus left 40 men behind on the island. He took some captive Native Americans with him. He landed in Spain in March 1493. Columbus was given a royal welcome for he had made a startling discovery to encourage trade. After his first voyage, Columbus made four more voyages, where he likewise discovered South and Central America but never a shorter route to Asia. He was now rich and well respected. But after his fourth voyage he had become weak. He died in 1506.

Christopher Columbus had discovered the New World by mistake but he was the only man who was brave enough to go into the unknown. He showed the path that the others followed. He was the first man and a courageous and determined explorer who made communication between the known and the unknown possible.

Let's remember the story

Answer the following questions.

1. What was the ambition of Columbus?
2. Why was the time in which Columbus lived called exciting?
3. What did he learn in Lisbon?
4. Who agreed to help Columbus? Why?
5. Why did the sailors rebel? Did they turn back?
6. What new places had Columbus found? What places did Columbus think he had found?

Antonyms

Can you match the words and their antonyms given in the following table?

Words	Antonyms
Captive	Disagree
Present	Coward
Rich	Die
Born	Absent
Agree	Poor
Courageous	Free

Think and fill

Fill in the blanks using the correct articles, *a*, *an* and *the*.

1. Sara is carrying .... present, ... cap and flowers.

2. .... sky is filled with dark clouds.

3. It is .... oldest building in our town.

4. Do you see .... boy in the blue shirt over there?

5. It will take us .... hour to reach the coast.

6. .... amazing thing happened to me today.

7. He lives in .... United States.

8. .... Amazon flows through .... rainforest.

Sea words

Given below are the words related with sailors and ships. Read them carefully and fill the sentences with the words.

knots	crow's nest	sailors	port	captain	
map	anchor	sails	compass	deck	direction

1. The ship is standing in the.............

2. The............... are keeping the supplies into the ship.

3. The ship's.......................... is looking at the.............

4. The sailor in the.................................... is keeping a look out.

5. The captain is looking at the........................... to know the ship's........................

6. A ship's speed is measured in.............................

7. The sailors are untying the ship's........................

8. The......................... has been kept on the ship's....................

Explore more!

Find out more about Columbus' voyage and learn about what other adventures he had. Your teacher can guide you about the places that he discovered.

Fun to Know

A warming up discussion
- Do you like rain?
- What is it that you like to do when there is rain?

A Rain Song

Tinkle, tinkle,

Lightly fall

On the peach buds, pink and small;

Tip the tiny grass, and twinkle

On the clover, green and tall.

Tinkle, tinkle,--

Faster now,

Little rain-drops, smite and sprinkle

Cherry-bloom and apple-bough!

Pelt the elms, and show them how

You can dash!

And splash! splash! splash!

While the thunder rolls and mutters,

And the lightnings flash and flash!

Then eddy into curls

Of a million misty swirls,

And thread the air with silver, and embroider it with pearls!

And patter, patter, patter

To a quicker time, and clatter

On the streaming window-pane;

Rain, rain,

On the leaves,

And the eaves,

And the turning weather-vane!

Rush in torrents from the tip

Of the gable-peak, and drip

In the garden-bed, and fill

All the cuckoo-cups, and pour

More and more

In the tulip-bowls, and still

Overspill

In a crystal tide until

Every yellow daffodil

Is flooded to its golden rim, and brimming o'er and o'er!

Then as gently as the low

Muffled whir of robin wings,

Or a sweep of silver strings,

Even so,

Take your airy April flight

Through the merry April light,

And melt into a mist of rainy music as you go!

(Evaleen Stein)

Complete the sentences

Read the sentences given below and complete them with the help of the poem.

1. Little rain-drops .... dash!
2. And splash! .... flash!
3. And patter, ... window-pane.
4. In a crystal .... o'er!
5. Then .... strings.
6. Even so .... you go!

It is a rainy day. What do you like to do when it rains? Do you enjoy it! Tell us how you would like to spend a rainy day.

....

....

....

....

....

....

....

....

....

 **Synonyms**

Match the words with their synonyms given in the following table.

Words	Synonyms
Small	Drizzle
Fast	Fog
Drip	Complain
Gentle	Little
Mist	Quick
Mutter	Docile

 **A budding writer!**

Write a short story on Dave's adventures on a rainy day. You can use the given words in your story.

| rain   play   football   raincoat   dislike   umbrella   wet   enjoy   friends |

Fun to Know

A warming up discussion
- Do you spend time with your family?
- Why do you like your family?

As Food Needs Salt

Characters

Narrator   King   Eldest Princess   Second Princess
Youngest Princess   Head Cook   Prince

Script

Narrator: Once upon a time, a king had three beautiful daughters. He, however, loved his youngest daughter the most. One day, he called his three daughters and their fiancés.

King: I have grown old. I cannot run the kingdom anymore. So I have decided to divide my kingdom among you.

Youngest Princess: Father, I find you capable enough to be a king.

King: You are being kind, my dear. But I have made my decision. After dividing my kingdom, I will stay with you three in turns. I shall, however, divide my kingdom based on how much you three love me.

Narrator: Everyone became silent. Then, the king asked his eldest daughter.

King: How much do you love me, my dear?

Eldest Princess: More than my own life, father.

Second Princess: Father, I love you more than anybody else in the whole world.

Youngest Princess: Father, I love you as a daughter should love a father and I need you as the food needs salt.

Narrator: Hearing this, the king was disappointed and angry with his youngest daughter. At once, he divided the kingdom among his elder daughters and banished the Youngest Princess. Instantly, her fiancé too left her as she was now poor.

Narrator: With a heavy heart, the Youngest Princess left the palace. Soon, she reached the neighbouring kingdom. Now, she needed money to support herself. By chance, she got work in the king's kitchen.

Narrator: Meanwhile, the old king now lived at the castle of her elder daughter. He had many servants to look after him. Due to his servants, the king's elder daughter was getting irritated and asked the old king to dismiss them.

King: My dear, I gave you my kingdom and you can't keep the men who serve me. If you cannot keep me, I shall leave immediately for my second daughter's home.

Narrator: But when he reached his second princesses' castle, she already knew what had happened. She too refused to keep her father if he brought along his servants. The King was disappointed.

Narrator: The king then wandered a while with his servants. Soon, he dismissed them. The king was now a poor man. He even began living in a small hut by the woods.

Meanwhile...

Head Cook: The prince is going to organize a grand feast. We must prepare ourselves. New girl, you must go and bring some herbs from the woods.

Narrator: The youngest princess while collecting herbs saw her old father, now poor, at the edge of the woods. She felt sorry for him. She went up to him but the old king did not recognize her.

Youngest Princess: Sir, do you live here alone?

King: Yes. Who would want to take care of an old man?

Youngest Princess: I would. I would come to meet you each day. But, now I must return to the palace.

Narrator: Back at the palace, she learnt that the prince had invited everyone to the feast. So excited, the princess wore a beautiful gown she had brought along and went to the grand feast. Nobody could recognize her. The prince too thought that she was a princess who has come from a distant land. He did not realise that she was the same princess he had left when she had become poor. After the feast, she quickly went away leaving the prince wondering who she was. Next morning...

Youngest Princess: Where is everyone going?

Head Cook: The prince is sending soldiers to search the princess who had come to the feast last night.

Youngest Princess: Which princess!

Head Cook: She was the most beautiful princess. Also, the prince says that he knows who she is but could not recognize her.

Youngest Princess: Perhaps, I can help the prince.

Narrator: Saying so, the princess prepared food for the prince. No sooner had he started eating the food that he called the Head Cook and the other cooks as well.

Prince: Who had cooked the food this morning?

Youngest Princess: I had prepared your food, Your Highness!

Prince: Then, tell me how did you got hold of this ring, I found in my food?

Youngest Princess: Someone gave it to me.

Prince: It looks to me that you are hiding something. Speak the truth.

Narrator: It was only then that she told him who she was. The prince was surprised to see her and was ashamed of his behaviour towards her.

Prince: Please forgive me for my behaviour, princess?

Narrator: Later, with the prince's help the old king was brought to the palace. He was treated as a king. Soon, he sat eating a lavish dinner. When...

Prince: Is the food not good, Your Majesty?

Old king: This food has no salt.

Youngest Princess: Here, is some salt, father.

Narrator: The old man looked up and seeing his youngest daughter his eyes filled with tears.

King: Please forgive me, my dear. I was blinded by my vanity and foolishness. I understand now that I am as important to you as salt is to make food delicious.

Youngest princess: I am glad to have my father back, Your Majesty!

Narrator: Soon, the youngest princess was married to her fiancé and the old king lived with them. He was now happy.

The End

 **Let's remember the story**

Answer the following questions.

1. What had the king decided to do?
2. Why did the king banish his youngest daughter?
3. In what manner did the princess earn her food?
4. How were the king's elder daughters ungrateful?
5. In what circumstances did the prince recognize the princess?
6. The old king realized that he had been vain. How?

 **Circling the words**

Read the passage given below. Circle all the describing words or adjectives in the passage.

Mars, also known as the Red Planet, is the fourth planet from the sun. Its red colour is because of the high amounts of iron oxide on its surface. Its surface is similar to the surface of the Earth and the Moon. It is, however, smaller than the Earth. Like the Earth, it has long mountain ranges, fiery volcanic fields, valleys, thick ice caps, deep canyons and vast deserts. It has numerous impact craters on its surface including the largest crater that is thousands of miles in length and breadth.

Mars is also home to Olympus Mons, the highest volcano in the solar system. Valles Marineris is also the largest canyon and it is more than seven miles deep. Do you know Mars has fearful dust storms that can sometimes cover the whole planet!

Think and fill

Fill in the blanks using the correct articles, *a*, *an* and *the*.

1. .... owl is sitting on .... tree branch.

2. .... girl is wearing .... raincoat.

3. Will you go to .... party?

4. Sofia got .... pup as her birthday present.

5. .... tiger can swim in .... water.

6. .... robbers took away all .... money.

7. Mother is baking .... apple cake.

8. .... gardener is planting .... orange and .... pear tree.

Words and their meanings

Read the words given below. With the help of a dictionary find out their meanings and write in the table.

Words	Meanings
Capable	
Glad	
Dismiss	
Feast	
Recognize	
Banish	

Plan a skit!

Prepare a small skit on the story, 'The Honest Woodcutter.' The teacher can write the script and help the children to enact the story.

Fun to Know

A warming up discussion
- What are rocks?
- Do you know where gemstones come from?

Gems and Minerals

You know that our Earth is made up of rocks. You also must have seen different types of rocks around yourself. Have you ever thought of how rocks are formed? Do you have any ideas? Rocks all over the world are formed of something called minerals.

Minerals are the building blocks of rocks. They are inorganic substances, i.e. non-living, which are found on the Earth. The rocks are made up of one or more minerals. Without minerals there would be no rocks. Think of it this way: You have to make lemonade. You need water, lemons, salt and sugar to make lemonade. When you mix them together what you get is lemonade. Similarly, rocks need minerals to form.

Do you know that people who study rocks, called geologists, have discovered more than 3000 minerals! Each of these minerals have their own chemical qualities. These particular qualities give the minerals their own unique shape, colour, shine and also tell us how hard or soft a particular mineral is.

Interestingly, the shape that the mineral takes in a rock is called a crystal. Crystals can be of various colours and can vary on its shine. Each crystal also has a distinct pattern. Some of the crystals formed by the minerals are precious. So sometimes these crystals are cut and polished and they then become gemstones or gems. The gems are then used to make jewellery or are used as decorative objects.

Crystals are chosen to make gems based on how beautiful they are and sometimes how rarely they occur. Diamonds, rubies, sapphires, emerald, quartz and amethysts are some of the gemstones formed from crystals. Emerald, sapphire and gold are some of the minerals that are difficult to find as they are found in only a few places on the Earth.

Do you know that crystals become gems under very extreme pressure deep inside the Earth! It takes a long time for the gems to form under the Earth. Interestingly, it is not an easy task to take out gems from under the Earth. Mining is the process through which we take out gems from the Earth. Do you know that coal and amber are not made up of minerals? Coal is formed from the decomposed plant matter while amber is the hardened form of ancient tree sap.

Though, man has always been interested in gems but the popularity of gems has varied from time to time. Ancient Greeks preferred amethyst. Today, we prefer gold and diamonds. Do you know that diamond is the hardest substance in the world? It is not only used as jewellery but is also used as a tool to cut and polish.

Over the years some diamonds have become world famous. Koh-i-Noor, found in India is among the largest diamonds in the world, the Hope Diamond which is thought to be cursed and Tiffany's Yellow Diamond are among the most famous diamonds in the world.

But diamonds too are only a gem formed out of minerals deep inside the Earth. Thus, it is right to say that we need minerals to make rocks but we do not require rocks to make minerals.

Let's remember the story

Answer the following questions.

1. What are minerals?
2. Name some qualities of minerals.
3. What is a crystal? How are they formed?
4. Name a few gems. Write some of their properties.
5. In what manner are coal and amber made?
6. Which is the hardest substance in the world? What is it used for?

Pick the correct answer

Choose the correct answers from the multiple choices given.

1. Who are geologists?
    a. People who read maps
    b. People who study only geometry
    c. People who study rocks
    d. People who like to go out

2. Ancient Greeks liked .... the most.

   a. Silver

   b. Sapphire

   c. Ruby

   d. Amethyst

3. Rocks are made up of one or more ....

   a. Vitamins

   b. Proteins

   c. Minerals

   d. Building blocks

4. Koh-i-Noor is the world's largest ....

   a. Amethyst

   b. Diamond

   c. Rock

   d. Pearl

Crossword

With the help of given clues, complete the crossword.

Down
1. An inorganic material that exists naturally inside the Earth
2. A black, hard substance that can be burned
3. A large mass of stone

Across
4. Hardest substance on Earth which is also a precious stone
5. Our planet
6. A person who studies rocks

Idioms

A group of words which has a different meaning compared to the written/spoken words is an idiom. Match the idioms given in Column A with their meanings in Column B.

Idioms	Meanings
A dime a dozen	Talking nonsense or a meaningless speech
Against the clock	Something which is common and easy to get
Hit the sack	To get married
Mumbo Jumbo	To be short on time
On the fence	To go to sleep
Tie the knot	Someone who is unable to decide

Be a geologist!

A list of gemstones is given below. Find out their pictures using the Internet and paste them in your notebooks.

diamond   amethyst   sapphire   emerald   ruby   topaz

Fun to Know

12

A warming up discussion
- Do you believe in magic?
- What would you like to do the most if you could do magic?

The Magic Brocade

Long ago, there lived an old widow with her son Chen in China. The old widow wove beautiful brocades to make a living. So much so that the brocades she wove were always sought after.

One day while returning home she stopped at a shop for there hung a beautiful painted scroll. It showed a marvellous palace amid the mountains.

'Oh my! What a beautiful picture!' she exclaimed.

'Do you like it?' asked the shopkeeper. 'It's a painting of the Sun Palace. People say that it is the home of fairies.'

The next moment, she bought the scroll without a second thought. Once home, she showed the painting to Chen who suggested that she should make it on her brocade.

So the widow set up her loom and began to weave. But it was no easy task to weave the painting onto the brocade. The widow wove for hours at the loom for many weeks. She spent little time to eat and rest.

Meanwhile, as the widow worked on the loom all day, Chen sold firewood to make their living. Weeks turned into months as inch by inch the pattern on the loom took its shape.

One day, when Chen came home in the evening, he saw that the loom was empty and his mother was crying, bitterly.

'What's wrong, mother?' he asked alarmed.

'Chen, I have completed the brocade at last!' she said tearfully, pointing to the brocade lying on the floor. It was his mother's finest work.

'It looks so wonderfully real,' said Chen amazed.

Suddenly, a strong gust of wind whipped through the cottage. It, at once, lifted the brocade, blew it out of the window and carried it through the air. The widow and Chen rushed outside to get the brocade but it was all in vain.

'It's gone!' cried the old woman bitterly. Chen was worried and went after the brocade.

Minutes later, Chen was heading towards the east. He walked for days and weeks. But there was no sign of the brocade. One day, Chen saw an old woman sitting outside a lonely hut. A horse grazed nearby. 'Hello, dear!' said the woman.

'Are you looking for the brocade of the Sun Palace! Well, the wind that came to your house was sent by the fairies of the Sun Palace. They are using the brocade as a pattern for their weaving.'

'But my mother will die without it!'

'Well, in that case, take my horse and it shall take you to the Sun Palace,' said the woman. 'On your way, you must pass through the flames of the Fiery Mountain. If you utter a single word of complaint, you'll be burnt to ashes. And then, there is the Icy Sea. The smallest word of discontent and you'll be frozen to solid ice.'

'I shall start immediately,' said Chen. 'Thank you for your help.'

Saying this, Chen climbed up the horse and soon he was galloping away. Chen found everything as the woman had said. But he let out no complaint. At last, he stood before the magnificent Sun Palace. Filled with admiration, Chen cautiously entered the palace. Inside, he reached a large hall where several fairies were sitting at their looms. He also saw his mother's brocade hanging in the middle of the hall and that the fairies had copies of the brocade kept beside their looms. When the fairies saw Chen, they stopped working. Then, a fairy got up and greeted Chen.

'My name is Li-en. I welcome you to the Sun Palace. Tell me, why are you here?'

But Chen was so taken aback by her beauty that he kept staring at her and didn't reply. At length, he said, 'Dear lady, I have come for my mother's brocade.'

'How we admire your mother's brocade! We wish to keep it here,' she said.

'But I must take it home or my mother will die!' said Chen anxiously.

Li-en looked alarmed and at once a flurry of whispers arose in the room. The fairies decided to finish the brocade overnight, so that Chen could take it home to his mother. As Chen rested, the fairies one by one completed their individual brocades.

Li-en was the last one to finish her weaving.

'Mine is good, but hers is brilliant! If only she could teach us,' she sighed.

Then, Li-en had an idea. With a needle and thread, she embroidered a small image of herself standing on the palace steps onto the widow's brocade. She then softly said a spell before leaving the hall. When Chen woke up, the next morning, he grabbed his mother's brocade and rushed out of the hall. Soon, his horse carried him over the Icy Sea and the Fiery Mountain.

Once again, he met the old woman outside her hut. He thanked her and then rushed to meet his mother. Soon, he was home. He rushed inside and saw his mother lying on her bed, pale and worn out.

'Mother!' he cried. The widow slowly opened her eyes and said weakly, 'Chen!'

'Mother, I have brought your brocade!'

'My brocade!' said the widow. The next moment, colour rushed back to her face and she looked stronger!

'Chen, I need more light to see it properly. Let's take it outside.'

Once outside, Chen placed the brocade on a rock. Just then, a sudden wind came and the brocade rose up slowly in the air. It grew larger and larger until it was the size of the real Sun Palace! Before the palace stood fairy Li-en! She called to them saying, 'Quick! Step into the brocade!'

For a moment, Chen was too shocked to move. Then he supporting his mother took a step. A shimmering light surrounded them, as they stepped forward and then they were standing outside the Sun Palace.

Li-en rushed to greet them along with the other fairies. The fairies said to the widow, 'Welcome, honoured one. Please stay with us and teach us how to weave beautiful brocades.'

'Nothing could please me more' said the old woman.

So the old woman became a teacher to the fairies and Chen got married to the beautiful Li-en. And together at the Sun Palace they lived for many years.

Let's remember the story

Answer the following questions.

1. What was painted on the scroll?

2. What did Chen suggest his mother to weave?

3. The brocade flew out of the window. Where did it go and why?

4. What did Chen see when he entered the Sun Palace?

5. What did Li-en do when she saw the old woman's brocade?

6. What did happen when Chen placed the brocade on the rock?

Words and their meanings

Read the words given below. With the help of a dictionary find out their meanings and write in the table.

Words	Meaning
Scroll	
Marvellous	
Loom	
Firewood	
Admire	
Weave	

Prepositions

Fill in the blanks using the prepositions given below.

| next to   for   on   in   beside   since   under   towards |

1. Mother bought a dozen mangoes .... me.

2. Nadia is standing .... the queue.

3. The wet dog has taken shelter .... the bridge.

4. The train is moving .... the platform.

5. The bird is sitting .... the fountain.

6. Sofia kept her shoes .... the shoe rack.

7. Jim stood .... Jerry in the photograph.

8. Alex has been playing .... morning.

81

Practise writing sentences

Use the following words in your own sentences.

1. Beautiful

   ....
   ....

2. Firewood

   ....
   ....

3. Work

   ....
   ....

4. Lonely

   ....
   ....

5. Empty

   ....
   ....

6. Loom

   ....
   ....

Fun to Know

A warming up discussion
- Do you use a phone to call people?
- Have you seen old phones? What were they like?

Telephone

You must have used a telephone a number of times. But have you ever thought who first invented it and how it was made! Well, the telephone was first invented by Alexander Graham Bell. He was a scientist and an inventor. He was born in Scotland on March 3, 1847. Even as a kid, Bell was interested in the manner sound was produced.

Once he even made his dog say, 'Ow ah oo ga ma ma.' His audience was astonished as what the dog said sounded like, 'How are you grandmamma?' He had done so by moving the voice box of the dog. That was perhaps his first experiment with sound. Growing up, he studied human sounds and also worked with various schools of the deaf. When he grew up, he invented the harmonic telegraph. Through this device one could send multiple messages over a single wire. But it was the invention of the telephone that made him famous.

After inventing the telegraph, which was a successful means of communication, Bell began to further improve it. By now, he had found two investors, Mr Sanders and Mr Hubbard, who gave him the money he needed to further experiment with the telegraph.

Along with his assistant Thomas Watson, who was an electrician, he worked with tuning forks, wires, batteries and electro-magnets to improve the telegraph. But all their efforts were not successful. Then, Bell thought of sending sound or speech over the telegraph wire. And he wanted to do so by using electricity. This idea had come in his mind during his experiments. Up till now, he had not shared his idea with Mr Sanders and Mr Hubbard. When he did tell them, they said that he should concentrate on sending multiple messages through the telegraph and not speech sounds.

Bell, however, had decided to send sound or speech over the wire. He also asked Mr Watson to help him in his work. He tried and tried. At last, he succeeded in sending vibrations from one room to the other. This success encouraged him. But when he tried to send sound, nothing was heard in the other room. Then, Bell and Watson thought of adding another transmitter to their device.

So they added a transmitter. They made this transmitter using wire and connected it to a metal cup which was filled with diluted sulphuric acid. As he continued to experiment, he finally achieved success on March 10, 1876. It was the day that telephone was born. As he was experimenting with Watson in the other room, he heard a sound that came from the other room over the wire as Watson worked on the device. Bell was delighted. He then said the famous words, 'Mr. Watson -- come here -- I want to see you.'

Watson heard his voice over the wire and that was the first telephone call. Bell and Watson had succeeded. Without wasting time, he rushed to the patent office to have this invention to his name. On the same day, another inventor Elisha Gray too had submitted a patent that covered that he had succeeded in transmitting speech using electricity. Bell and Gray fought a long battle in court. But in the end, Bell won as he was the first to submit the patent for a telephone.

Thus, the telephone was invented. With time, Bell started his telephone company. In a short time, telephone had become a highly successful invention worldwide. Interestingly, Alexander Graham bell did not keep a telephone in his study at his home as the telephone disturbed him. Little did he know how much his invention of the telephone would change the future of communication!

Complete the sentences

Read the sentences given below and complete them with the help of the chapter.

1. Alexander Bell made his dog say ....

2. Alexander needed these things to improve the telegraph.

   ....

   ....

3. He made a transmitter using ....

   ....

   ....

   ....

4. Bell said the famous words ....
   ....
   ....
   ....

5. Bell did not keep phone in his study room because ....
   ....
   ....
   ....

6. Little did Bell know how much ....
   ....
   ....
   ....

Think and fill

Fill in the blanks using the correct *a, an*, and *the*.

1. I have just had............ great idea.
2. He was going 90 miles........... hour on............ highway.
3. Did you read.......... book I gave you?
4. Dancing is............ interesting activity.
5. This is......... man I told you about.
6. I haven't been to......... concert before.
7. It's........... long way to the railway station.
8. Where have you kept............ scissors?

Dialogue writing

Write a short dialogue between you and your friend. Your friend is inviting you to attend his/her birthday party. Write another dialogue where you are asking your brother/sister to help you with your school work.

Put on a detective's shoes!

Alexander Graham Bell made the first telephone. But telephone has changed a lot with the passage of time. Find out under your teacher's guidance how first calls were made on the telephone. Also find out how telephones have changed.

Word steps

Read the word 'Telephone' given below on the first step of the ladder. Now, you must write five more words on the remaining steps. Remember that each new word must begin with the last letter of the previous word.

Telephone

| Step 1 |
| Step 2 |
| Step 3 |
| Step 4 |
| Step 5 |
| Step 6 |

Fun to Know

A warming up discussion
- Do you know about dragons? What were they like?
- Do you think dragons were real?

The Boy and the Dragon

Once, long ago, a boy lived with his parents in a village near the ocean. He longed for adventure and companionship. He had decided to seek his fortune elsewhere when he heard that a great dragon had come there. The dragon caused great havoc. People were terrified because the dragon could change his form into a human. In his human form, the dragon caught his victims, took them to his house in the forest and ate them.

The boy thought, 'Here is my chance to do a great deed.' So after saying farewell to his parents, he went in search of this form-changing dragon. He travelled all day. By evening, he had come to a high hill in the centre of an open space. He climbed the hill. As he stood at the top of the hill, he saw a man standing beside him. The man was a charming fellow and they talked for some time.

Then, the stranger asked the boy, 'Where are you going?'

'I am going far away,' said the boy. 'I am seeking adventure in the forest for it is very lonely down by the sea.'

The boy cleverly did not tell the man his real purpose. Hearing this, the man said, 'You may stay with me tonight. You can rest and gain your strength.'

The boy was tired and hungry, so he went along with the man to his house. When they reached there, the boy saw a great heap of bleached bones lying before the door. But he showed no fear nor did he say anything on the horrible sight. Then, he saw a very old and bent woman,

tending a pot. Soon, the boy and the man had a delicious meal.

After they had eaten, the man went out to gather wood for the fire, and the boy sat talking to the old woman. The old woman said, 'You are very young and innocent. Therefore, I take pity on you and am warning you of the danger you are in. The man who brought you here is none other than the dragon-man. He cannot be killed in ordinary combat and it is foolish to try. Tomorrow he will kill you. But you can be saved. Take these moccasins, and in the morning when you get up put them on your feet. With one step you will reach the hill you see in the distance. Give this piece of birch bark with the picture on it to a man you will meet there, and he will tell you what next to do. But remember that no matter how far you go, the dragon-man will overtake you in the evening.'

The youth then took the moccasins and the birch bark and hid them under his coat, and said, 'I will do as you have advised.'

The youth went to sleep, and the dragon-man slept all night beside him to prevent his escape. The next morning, when the dragon-man was out to get water from the stream, the boy at once got up, placed the moccasins on his feet and with one great step he reached the distant hill. Here, he met an old man and gave him the piece of birch bark. The man looked at it closely, smiled and said, 'So it is you I was told to wait for. That is well.' Then, the man gave him another pair of moccasins in exchange for those he was wearing, and another piece of birch bark bearing another inscription. He pointed to a hill towards the horizon and asked him to go there.

The boy put the moccasins on his feet, and with one step he reached the distant hill. There he met another old man, who gave him another pair of moccasins and a large maple leaf bearing a strange symbol, and told him to go to another spot, where he would receive final instructions. At the said spot, he met a very old man, who said, 'Down there is a stream. Go towards it and walk straight into it, as if you were on dry ground. Do not look at the water. Take this piece of birch bark bearing these magic figures, and it will change you into whatever you wish, and it will keep you away from harm.'

The boy did as he was told. After crossing the stream, the boy followed it for some distance and towards evening he came to a lake. There, the boy saw the dragon-man hiding behind the trees in his original form. The old woman's words had come true. Quickly, the boy waved his magic bark and became a little fish with red fins, moving slowly in the lake.

Soon, the dragon-man came to the lake, saw the little fish and cried, 'Little fish of the red fins, have you seen the youth I am looking for?' 'No, sir,' said the little fish, 'I have seen no one; I have been asleep.' And he swam deep into the lake.

The dragon-man moved down along the bank of the lake, while the youth watched him from the water. The dragon-man met a Toad and asked, 'Little Toad, have you seen the youth I am looking for? 'I have not' answered the Toad and he hopped away into the moss. Then the

dragon-man saw a very large fish and he asked, 'Have you seen the boy I am looking for?' 'Yes,' said the fish, 'you have just been talking to him,' it said. The dragon-man went back and searched for the Toad but in vain. The dragon-man was deceived again. Then, he asked an old Turtle in the lake. 'You are old and wise,' he said, 'you must have seen the person I am looking for.'

'Yes,' said the Turtle, 'go across the river and you will find him. But beware, for if you do not know him when you see him, he will surely kill you.' The dragon-man soon came to the river. Then, he transformed into a snake and began to swim in the river. Boy, still in the form of a fish had seen him.

For some time, he had been swimming round and round in a circle in the middle of the river. A rapid whirlpool arose where he swam but it was not visible on the surface. In no time, unaware, the snake was caught in the whirlpool and drowned. The boy then took his original form and cut off the snake's head. Soon, the boy returned home and it became known that he had killed the dragon-man. He was greatly praised for his bravery and was hugely rewarded. And from that day, the land was not troubled by dragons anymore.

Let's remember the story

Answer the following questions.

1. Why were the people terrified?
2. How did the dragon-man kill his victims?
3. What did the boy see when he entered the house?
4. What advice did the old woman give the boy?
5. What did the boy turn into? What did the old turtle tell the dragon-man?
6. How did the boy kill the dragon-man?

Antonyms

Can you match the words and their antonyms given in the following table?

Words	Antonyms
Blame	Reveal
Apart	Host
Humble	Together
Conceal	Mild
Guest	Praise
Harsh	Proud

g Circling the words

Read the passage given below carefully and put a circle around the action words or verbs.

Today, Jimmy along with his mother went to the library. Jimmy wanted to read a book while his mother needed to use the computer there. In the library, soon Jimmy found a book about detectives. He began reading interestingly as the detective was looking for a friendly ghost. After a while, he carried the book in his hand and went looking for his mother.

Jimmy saw his mother sitting before one of the computer's at the library. She was searching on the Internet about gardening. She also looked for some flowers and wrote their names in her notebook. Jimmy saw that she had a book on gardening kept beside her bag. Seeing him, mother smiled. Minutes later, Jimmy and his mother were at the front desk. They got both the books issued for three weeks. Grinning from ear to ear, Jimmy and his mother went towards their car and soon were on their way home.

Word ladder

Let's make a word ladder. You can change one letter at each step and make a new word. All the words that you make should be of four letters only. Go on then, reach from Heap to Real.

HEAP

H _ _ _

_ _ _ D

R _ _ _

REAL

Words and their meanings

Read the words given below. With the help of a dictionary find out their meanings and write in the table.

Words	Meanings
Havoc	
Charming	
Transform	
Combat	
Distant	
Deceive	

Fun to Know

A warming up discussion
- Do you know where Russia is?
- Do you like winters? Why? If not, why?

King Frost

This story took place long, long ago in a far away country called Russia. There in a small village lived an old woman with her husband, her stepdaughter and her own daughter. The old woman was rude and wicked. Her own daughter was dear to her, and she always said praising words for her but for her stepdaughter, she had not even a kind word to say. In fact, the only time when she talked with her step daughter was to reproach her. Then, one day, the wicked old woman thought of a way to get rid of her stepdaughter. It was a very cold day when she went up to her husband.

She said, 'Now, old man, I want you to take your daughter out of my sight. But I do not want you to send her to your people in the warmer regions either. I want you to take her to the wide, wide fields of the crackling frost.'

Her husband was stunned to hear this. 'You cannot be so cruel,' he cried. 'Let me just leave her with my people if you don't want to see her.'

But the old woman would not agree to this. Disappointed, the old man prepared the sleigh and as tears rolled down his eyes told his beloved daughter where he was taking her.

Before, they started their journey, the man wished to cover his daughter with a sheepskin in order to protect her from the cold. But he dare not do so because of his wife. Then, with a heavy heart, he started the sleigh and they went towards the wide, wide fields. He drove her nearly to the woods. Once there, he looked at his daughter lovingly for a while then left her there alone before speedily driving away back to his house.

So alone, quite alone, the little girl stood by the woods. Then, broken-

hearted and terror-stricken she repeated fervently all the prayers she knew as she walked into the woods. Now King Frost lived in the woods. He was the almighty sovereign of that place. He was clad in furs, with a long, long, white beard and a shining crown on his white head. He had seen all that had happened at the edge of the woods. Curious, he approached nearer and nearer, looking at this beautiful little guest of his.

When he had reached the little girl, he smiled and asked, 'Do you know me?—me, the red-nosed Frost?'

'Yes, I do, King Frost,' answered the young girl gently. 'I hope our heavenly Lord sent you for my sinful soul.'

'Are you comfortable, sweet child?' again asked the Frost. He was exceedingly pleased with her looks and mild manners.

'Indeed I am,' answered the girl, though she was out of breath due to the cold.

All this while, King Frost, cheerful and bright, kept crackling in the branches around the little girl until the air became icy. Every now and then, King Frost kept asking her, how she was but the good-natured girl kept repeating that she was comfortable.

But King Frost, however, knew all about the weakness of human beings. He knew that only a few among them were really good and kind. He also knew that not one single human could struggle too long against the power of Frost, the king of winter. The kindness of the gentle girl charmed old Frost so much that he made the decision to treat her differently from others. Suddenly, he came towards the girl and gave her a large heavy trunk filled with many beautiful, beautiful things.

'My dear, I am impressed with your manners,' he said, as he gave her a long coat lined with precious furs. The girl stopped shivering and thanked King Frost. In the trunk, when she looked at it, she saw in it silk quilts—light like feathers and warm as a mother's lap. What a rich girl she became and how many magnificent garments there were in it!

Wearing the rich fur coat, she became the most beautiful maiden under the sun. Meanwhile, the maiden's stepmother was busy preparing for the girl's funeral as the father of the maiden sat crying in a corner. Seeing him, the woman said mercilessly, 'Stop crying, old man. Go down to the wide fields and bring the body of your daughter so we can bury her.'

With a heavy heart, the old man stepped outside.

Minutes later, somebody opened the door to their house and the old woman heard voices that were laughing and talking outside. As she looked out, she stood still in amazement. It was because her stepdaughter was standing at the door looking like a princess, bright and happy in the most beautiful garments. Behind her, her old husband stood carrying a heavy trunk.

The old woman was stunned when she learnt what had happened with her stepdaughter. She had only wanted her stepdaughter to die. Then, she suddenly got up and told her husband, 'Old man! Hitch our best horses to our best sleigh, and drive my daughter to the very same place in the wide, wide fields. I want her to have a better fate than your daughter.'

The old man obeyed as usual and took his stepdaughter to the same place and left her alone. Once again, King Frost saw all that happened at the edge of the woods. Once again, he came to greet his new guest.

'Are you comfortable, fair maiden?' asked the red-nosed sovereign.

'Leave me alone,' harshly answered the girl. 'Can you not see that my feet and hands are stiff from the cold?'

The Frost calmly kept crackling and asking the girl questions for quite a while, but not once did he obtain a polite answer. He became angry and froze the girl to death. Soon, the old woman sent her husband to get her daughter saying, 'Old man, go for my daughter. Be careful and do not lose the trunk.'

After a while, the old woman heard the sound of the sleigh. Eager to see her daughter dressed as a princess, she rushed outside but to her horror, she saw her daughter frozen stiff. She wept and wept. It was only then that she understood her envy and wickedness that has led to the death of her daughter.

Let's remember the story

Answer the following questions.

1. In what manner did the old woman treat his stepdaughter?
2. What did she tell her husband to do?
3. In what manner did Father Frost test the young girl?
4. What was the old woman preparing for?
5. Why was the old woman filled with amazement?
6. What happened to the old woman's daughter? Why?

Dialogue writing

Write a short dialogue between you and your father asking him to tell you how to plant seeds in your garden.

Idioms

Match the idioms given in Column A with their meanings in Column B.

Idioms	Meaning
Baker's dozen	To die
Kick the bucket	Something done in excess
Bite your tongue	For certain
On the fence	Thirteen
Over the top	To stop or avoid talking
Without a doubt	To be undecided

Word steps

Read the word 'Frost' given below on the first step of the ladder. Now, you must write five more words on the remaining steps. Remember that each new word must begin with the last letter of the previous word.

Frost

Step 1
Step 2
Step 3
Step 4
Step 5
Step 6

Widen your horizon

Locate Siberia on a globe or a map. Find out about its atmosphere, people and animals. Then share what you have found out in groups with your classmates.

Fun to Know

16 A warming up discussion
- Would you like to keep a bird as a pet?
- How would you care for it?

The Tongue-cut Sparrow

Once upon a time there lived an old man and an old woman. The old man was kind-hearted. He also kept a young sparrow, which he tenderly nurtured. But the old woman was wicked and never liked the sparrow. One day, the old woman put out some paste which she wanted to use to starch her linen. As she kept the paste, a few drops of it fell on the ground. The sparrow seeing the drops flew to peck at them. Seeing, the sparrow pecking, the woman became very angry. In her anger, she cut off the sparrow's tongue and then let it loose. The poor sparrow flew away to the forest.

In the evening, the old man returned and searched for his sparrow among the tree branches. But the sparrow was nowhere to be seen. Anxious, he asked where his sparrow was. At once, the old woman said, 'The sparrow has flown away. It tried to peck at the starch I had kept outside, so I cut off its tongue and let it go.' When the old man heard this cruel tale, he was filled with grief. He thought, 'Where can my poor bird be? Poor thing! Poor little tongue-cut sparrow! I must find my bird.' Thinking thus, he walked out of his house and went into the forest. At intervals, he kept crying, 'Mr. Sparrow! Mr. Sparrow! Where are you living?'

He wandered into the forest for many days. Then, one day, at the foot of a certain mountain, the old man met his lost sparrow. How happy they were to see each other! As they talked, the sparrow invited the old man to his house. Once at the sparrow's house, the old man was introduced to the sparrow's wife and chicks. He then set before the old man all sorts of dainties, and entertained him hospitably.

He stayed at the sparrow's house for a few days. At last the old man said, 'My dear sparrow, I must return home now. I am glad to see that you are happy.' 'Just wait a moment before you go,' said the sparrow and went inside his house. He returned with two boxes. The sparrow begged the old man to carry them with him as a parting present. As the old man looked, he saw that one of the box was bigger and heavier, and the other was smaller and lighter. Then, he said, 'I am feeble and stricken in years. I shall, therefore, accept only the smaller box.' Saying so, he took the box, and trudged off towards his home.

Later, seeing him, the old woman became very angry, and began to scold him saying, 'Well, and pray where have you been all these days?'

'Oh!' replied he, 'I had been on a visit to the sparrows; and when I came away, they gave me this box as a parting gift.' Seeing the box, the old woman was in a hurry to open it. And, lo and behold, it was full of gold and silver and precious things. When the old woman, who was as greedy as she was cross, saw all the riches before her, she could not contain her joy.

'I'll go and call upon the sparrows, too,' said she. The old man understood his wife's intention hearing this. She then asked the old man the way to the sparrows' house, and started her journey next morning.

Soon, the old woman reached the sparrow's house. 'Well met! Well met, Mr. Sparrow! I have been looking forward to the pleasure of seeing you,' she said trying to impress the sparrow. The sparrow knew that the old woman was only pretending to be nice but he invited her to her house.

But unlike the old man, the sparrow did not prepare a feast for the woman nor did he intend to give her a parting gift. She, however, was not to be put off. So the old woman asked for something to carry away with her in remembrance of her visit to the sparrows. The sparrow, as he had done before, produced two boxes. At once, the greedy woman took the heavier basket and after saying her goodbyes went towards her home. Once home, she opened the basket to see what was inside. But instead of gold and jewels, all sorts of flies came out, encircled her and in no time she was not seen again.

 **Let's remember the story**

Answer the following questions.

1. In what manner did the old woman want to use the paste?
2. Why did she cut the sparrow's tongue?
3. Where did the old man found the sparrow? What happened next?
4. What did the sparrow give the old man as a parting gift? What was in it?
5. Why did the old woman want to meet the tongue-cut sparrow?
6. What happened to the old woman when she opened the basket?

 **Words and their meanings**

Read the words given below. With the help of a dictionary find out their meanings and write in the table.

Words	Meaning
Wicked	
Grief	
Humble	
Feeble	
Greed	
Impress	

Practise writing sentences

Use the following words in your own sentences.

1. Ground

   ....
   ....

2. Cruel

   ....
   ....

3. Lost

   ....
   ....

4. Polite

   ....
   ....

5. Pretty

   ....
   ....

6. Invite

   ....
   ....

Prefixes and suffixes

Given below are a few prefixes and suffixes along with a number of words. Use them together to make new words.

-ness	in-	-able	un-
comfort	do	finite	port
pack	action	visible	equal
happy	afford	eat	polite
lucky	usual	correct	kind
stead	security	move	notice

....

....

....

....

....

Fun to Know

17 **A warming up discussion**
- What is an island?
- Can you think of a city or a country that is built by joining small islands through bridges and canals?

Venice

How many bridges and canals have you seen? The numbers you would say would always be less than how many bridges and canals the city of Venice has. Venice is the most amazing and beautiful city in the world. What makes this city unique is that it is not built on land. Venice is built in water!

Venice is located in the lagoon at the mouths of the Rivers Po and Piave. The city is made up of 118 islands put together. All these islands are connected to each other through bridges. Do you know that there are more than 400 bridges in Venice? That is not all as Venice has about 200 canals. These canals have been around since 5th century AD and that is a long time back. The Grand Canal is the biggest canal in Venice. It is a S-shaped canal and is good way to see the city. It also divides Venice into two sections. As the city is in water, the main mode of transportation is through boats called gondolas. Though Venice has a train station but there are cars or bikes in the city as well. Water taxis and boats will take you all across Venice.

But its canals and bridges are not the only things unique to Venice. The city is also the city of art. The city has a wide collection of beautiful buildings. As one passes along the Grand Canal, one sees on either side of the canal, grand architectural buildings that speak of the richness of the culture of Venice. The city also has many museums, lively squares and magnificent churches and palaces that hold one's attention.

Venice came into being during the 5th century AD. During that time, the Venetian population that lived on the mainland was greatly troubled by the barbarians who had come to destroy them. So in order to escape them, the Venetian came to these islands. The Barbarians could not come here so the people were saved. But they did not return and stayed on the islands. With time more people came and that is how Venice came into being.

Venice is divided into 6 sections called sestieri across the Grand Canal. But that is not all that is to Venice. Venice is also known for its festivals and carnivals. The Venice Carnival is world famous. During this 12 day celebration, the Venetians spend fun willed days. They dress up in costumes and wear masks than join in parades, parties and what not. Do you know the masks worn in this carnival are also available for tourists! Redentore Regatta is an important festival and all the celebrations take place along the Grand Canal.

But being a city on water also has its disadvantages. Do you know that each year Venice has two months long floods! Though the Venetians are used to the flood but they still face problems. In recent years, the floods have become worse. Some even say that Venice is slowly sinking. But it is still a long way in future. Still, however, there is no denying the fact that Venice is one of the most beautiful and amazing cities in the world. Each year, thousands of tourists come to Venice to experience the grandeur of this city. And they cannot help but say that this city has come out of a fairy tale.

So why not take a ride in a gondola and move slowly among the many twisting canals of Venice. Take a walk along the streets of the city, eat the delicious food at the numerous cafes and explore the rich culture of Venice. Undoubtedly, Venice is the most beautiful city in the world.

Let's remember the story

Answer the following questions.

1. What is the main mode of transport in Venice?
2. Write a few lines about the Grand Canal.
3. How and why did people come to Venice?
4. Where is Venice located?
5. What is the city of Venice like?
6. Why do people say that Venice is sinking?

Prepositions

Fill in the blanks using the prepositions given below.

| beside | in | about | to | on | inside | over | after |

1. Tom told me............ his trip to New York.
2. The cat jumped................ the fence.
3. I sat.................. George in the stadium.
4. Tuesday comes................... Monday.

5. He saw the thief hiding.................. that building.
6. Our pet dog often sits............. the sofa.
7. The fruits are kept........... the basket.
8. He took a bus............ the store.

Synonyms

Match the words with their synonyms given in the following table.

Words	Synonyms
Eager	Hard
Dare	Remove
Furious	Control
Harsh	Challenge
Manage	Angry
Omit	Keen

Dialogue writing

Write a short dialogue between you and your brother/sister where each of you talk about a surprise party that you want to organise for your parents.

Everyone is invited!

You must like to party and go there dressed up. So would it not be interesting to know about one of the biggest parties on Earth! Find out with your teacher's help about the Venice Carnival, about why it was started, when it takes place and for how long it is celebrated. Write what you learn in a small paragraph.

Fun to Know

18 A warming up discussion
- What is the Earth's crust made of?
- Do you know a place where you can see the Earth's crust?

Grand Canyon

Do you know how old our Earth is? Have you ever thought of how many layers are beneath the soil under your feet! Perhaps, if you will dig the ground all that you will see would be soil. But there are layers over layers that form the Earth's surface. And there is one place where you can see these layers that tell the fascinating story of billion years of the Earth's formation. This marvellous place is called the Grand Canyon.

The Grand Canyon is located in the United States. It is a canyon that had been formed over millions of years by the Colorado River. Though it is not the longest or the deepest canyon but it tells the tale of millions of years of the Earth's history. The Grand Canyon is 277 miles long and its width ranges from 4-18 miles. Over years and years, the Colorado River and its tributaries have cut through the various layers of the rock to form the canyon. The action of water has led to erosion which has exposed the Earth's layers for all to see.

Do you know that the Grand Canyon became a national park in 1919! As the water cut through the rocks, it also uplifted the Colorado plateau. And today, the canyon is more than a mile deep. However, along with the rushing waters of the Colorado River, wind too has played a role to form the Grand Canyon. Each year, millions of visitors come to see the world at its grandest. Scientists spend a lot of time studying the layers of the Earth. Nowhere else on Earth are the Earth's layers seen so clearly so much so that they can tell about the Earth's layers. Even today, the Colorado River continues to change the shape of the Grand Canyon.

You will wonder if there are any plants or animals in the Grand Canyon. Interestingly, despite the harsh winters and the dry, humid summer weather that dominate the canyon, there is plenty of wildlife and vegetation. More than 1500 varieties of plants are found in the canyon. Interestingly, about 500 varieties of animals of various species are distributed in the canyon.

Do you know that the rocks at the bottom of the Grand Canyon are 2 billion years old! Often animal marks and some fossils have been seen on these layers but interestingly no fossil of any animal has been found. People, too, especially Native Americans have been living in the canyon for hundreds of years. Do you know that on the Havasupai reservation in the Grand Canyon, one can send mails only through the mules!

Though not the longest and the widest canyon, the Grand Canyon continues to draw visitors because of its beautiful landscape. It is only here that the Earth's history is well preserved in the ancient rocks on the walls of the canyon. But in recent times, rock falls has further widened the Grand Canyon. Interestingly, the Grand Canyon is higher at its northern rim than at its southern rim.

There are many things to discover in the Grand Canyon. One can go on foot, take to river rafting or perhaps gliding is your way to travel and explore. But no matter what option one takes, the Grand Canyon does not fail to impress you. Its immense size is unarguably the most recognizable landmark in the world.

# Complete the sentences

Read the sentences given below and complete them with the help of the chapter.

1. In the Grand Canyon you will see..
   ....

2. It has been formed by the action ....
   ....

3. The climate of Grand Canyon is ....
   ....
   ....

4. The Grand Canyon is famous because ....
   ....
   ....

5. One can see the Grand Canyon by ....
   ....
   ....

6. The Colorado river has cut ....
   and made the canyon ....
   ....

113

Pick the correct answer

Choose the correct answers from the multiple choices given.

1. Where is the Grand Canyon located?
    a. Mexico
    b. Egypt
    c. The United States
    d. Canada

2. In the Grand Canyon one can see
    a. The Earth's layers
    b. Water
    c. Sand
    d. Rocks

3. Which river flows through the Grand Canyon?
    a. The Nile
    b. The Colorado River
    c. The Mississippi
    d. The Amazon

4. .... have been living in the Grand Canyon.
    a. Amazons
    b. Native Americans
    c. Tribal people
    d. Zulus

Idioms

Match the idioms given in Column A with their meanings in Column B.

Idioms	Meanings
An arm and a leg	To carefully watch someone
Dry run	To have an enjoyable day
Field day	To do a rehearsal
Hit the books	To stop something suddenly
Keep an eye on him	Something very expensive
Pull the plug	To study

Know your planet

Do you know about the Earth's layers? How many layers are there? With the help of your teacher learn about the Earth's layers. You can later write what you have learnt in the space provided.

....

....

....

....

....

....

Rocks! Rocks! Rocks!

Rocks are of different kinds and types. Find about the Igneous, Sedimentary and Metamorphic Rocks. Name a few in each category and write a few lines about each kind of rocks.

1. Igneous

   ....

   ....

   ....

   ....

2. Sedimentary

   ....

   ....

   ....

   ....

3. Metamorphic

   ....

   ....

   ....

   ....